# My Marketing Miscellany

# My Marketing Miscellany

## Paul Rouse F.C.I.M.

*"This is not a textbook; it is aimed at marketing people on the way up with an eye to the main chance".*

**Paul Rouse**

© Paul Rouse 2010

Published by York Business Press

ISBN 978-0-9564804-0-8

A CIP catalogue record for this book is available from the British Library.

Cover and cartoons written by Paul Rouse and drawn by Mike Bryson

Prepared and printed by:

York Publishing Services Ltd
64 Hallfield Road
Layerthorpe
York YO31 7ZQ
Tel: 01904 431213
Website: www.yps-publishing.co.uk

*To my wife Joy, who has somehow put up with me for 40 years.*

# Contents

# Foreword

I have heard it argued that marketing people do not read books about how to be a good marketing manager/director - they have neither the time nor the need, because they are doing it already. Nevertheless, I am sure that you will find in these pages, as I did, and however busy you are, that Paul's tips and warnings, alongside a huge slice of common sense, are not only interesting and amusing, but also very helpful in a variety of situations.

The CIM Members' Benevolent Fund offers advice and financial support, on an entirely confidential basis, to members who find themselves confronting life-changing challenges - challenges which threaten their career, their homes, or their loved ones. To do this, the Fund relies on contributions from the CIM and donations from Branches, Industry Groups, and individuals.

Paul Rouse has offered to donate the proceeds from the sale of his book to the Benevolent Fund, and on behalf of the Trustees I thank him most sincerely for this extremely generous action. We look forward to hearing of world record sales for "My Marketing Miscellany!"

A.J.Beale
Chairman
Chartered Institute of Marketing Members' Benevolent Fund

# Introduction

I've had an interesting working life, although it didn't start that way in 1960.

My first job was in an advertising agency, as a 15 year old office junior earning just £1 per week, while attending night classes at the local art college. The job involved sending the wooden mounted printing plates used for advertisements, or blocks as they were known, to newspapers throughout the country. I'm easily bored, soon became fed up with packing the plates in corrugated paper, and so began sending them out in envelopes. Newspapers started to complain that they were arriving damaged, and I got my first, but by no means my last, bollocking for doing something the easy way.

As soon as someone gave me something interesting to do, my performance improved, and by age 18, I was Production Manager of a small ad agency.

At the same time, I earned twice as much, managing and playing bass guitar in a rock band.

However, a brief spell as a full time professional musician convinced me that I was probably a better advertising man than musician, and so at the age of 21, I applied for, and to my amazement I got, one of the top advertising jobs in the North of England at that time.

John Collier was a leading TV advertiser of the day, with a famous advertising jingle 'the window to watch'. It was a part of UDS Group, which was then the second largest retailer in Europe. The Chairman, Bernard Lyons, took an interest in me, and he taught me about 'business'. I quickly realised that the future for someone like me in the retail industry was to combine the then separate functions of advertising, shop design, display and merchandising into a single discipline - marketing.

I must have been doing something right because during my time at John Collier I was headhunted to join a Leeds based Company called Associated Dairies as Advertising Director of their retail division. My response was "what does a dairy know about retailing". It was of course ASDA, and dismissing their offer out of hand was just one of the many mistakes I made over the years.

I became a Member of the Institute of Marketing in 1969, and as I worked my way up the corporate ladder, I attended every one of their marketing seminars and workshops I could get my various employers to pay for.

At the age of 28, I achieved my ambition to become a Company Director, and joined the Board of the largest furniture retailer in Scotland as Marketing Director.

Over the next 25 years, I ran two Ad Agencies as Managing Director, and headed up the marketing functions at Allied Carpets, and William Hill. While at William Hill, I started a telecommunications Company that a colleague and I eventually bought and turned into a Public Company.

I learned a lot in 32 years, frequently by making mistakes. So, if this book helps a few people to avoid some of those, it'll be worthwhile. It is not a textbook; it is aimed at marketing people on the way up, who have an eye to the main chance. I have therefore tried not to fill a page for the sake of filling it, and although the anecdotes ramble at times, I hope they are worth reading.

**Paul Rouse**

# CHAPTER ONE

## Are Marketing people born or made?

IN MY OPINION POTENTIAL MARKETERS ARE BORN
WITH A CREATIVE MIND

"I do not believe that someone without any creative flair can become a good marketer."

# Are Marketing People Born or Made?

All good marketing people are creative, but the best instinctively know when an idea has legs.

However, when the stakes are high, even the most instinctive marketer may need to use a structured approach and supporting data, particularly if Board approval is needed (see PLANNING AND ANALYSIS Chapter) so an organised, as well as a creative, mind, comes in useful.

The really good ones are also numerate, and the very best are lucky.

I was fortunate enough to spend a large part of my career in a time when a marketing strategy and budget could be agreed, and I was then left to get on with it. If I got it right, life was very pleasant, if I got it wrong, people seemed to avoid me. Fortunately, I got it right most of the time.

I do recall one instance of getting it wrong in a big way. I had recently joined William Hill as head of marketing, and decided that the bookmaker's football coupons had the potential to broaden our market. I took full page ads on a Friday in the popular daily newspapers, using cartoons to illustrate the product, and had our odds compilers shave our prices to make the bets as attractive as possible. We lost £1million on football bets that weekend!

The Managing Director of William Hill at the time was not famed for his tolerance or patience, so I approached Monday morning with some trepidation. I was therefore not surprised to be summoned to his office, but very surprised to find him with a smile on his face. He told me that I had learned a valuable lesson. It seems that increasing betting turnover does not always result in increased profits. Get the odds wrong, and the increased turnover simply means larger losses. However, a good win for the punters can produce a knock on benefit. The punters tell their friends how much they won, and the business grows, generating profits in the longer term. Sure enough, the following weeks we did record football business, winning back what we had paid out, and gained a lot of extra customers.

That's a good example of being lucky, but I do not believe that someone without any creative flair can become a good marketer, however lucky they are.

When I joined Allied Carpets, the guy who had been in charge of marketing, and who had been promoted to CEO, did not have a creative bone in his body, yet thought his boring and methodical ads were the way to utilise the massive media spend. The fact that the Company was in trouble, and spent more on marketing than it made in trading profit, did not seem to bear that out, but somehow he had been given the top job. There followed three years of hell, during which time I fought hard to improve things, with some success, until our bust up, and my departure, became a matter of when, not if.

As a marketer gets older, creative instinct gradually gives way to analysis, or experience.

There is nothing wrong with that, as experience is a wonderful thing, but care must be taken not to stifle junior colleagues by dismissing ideas because they have been tried in the past. Things change and so it is best to use experience to guide and fine tune, rather than dismiss things out of hand. Obviously, it is wrong to spend time on really rotten ideas, just to avoid hurting someone's feelings, but people who come up with rotten ideas should not be in the marketing department.

I'm no great scholar, and, if recruiting for a marketing position, would be the last person to dismiss an applicant because he or she lacked formal qualifications. Having said that, some of the best marketers I employed, had a relevant qualification. Equally, many did not. However, they were all creative thinkers, even though it is not enough to be full of ideas.

I also felt that the best of them had a healthy respect for money, and wanted as much of it as possible.

*So, the answer to the question is that, in my opinion, marketers are born with a creative mind, but the really good ones combine creativity with numerousy and organisational ability, tinged with a little greed.*

# CHAPTER 2

## Preparing a marketing strategy plan

KEEP IT DOWN TO A MAXIMUM 10 SLIDE PRESENTATION OR YOU WILL LOSE YOUR AUDIENCE.

"There is no better time to get something radical approved than at the start of your tenure."

# Preparing a Marketing Strategy Plan

It is very easy to become immersed in the detail of an organisation and lose the big picture.

So, when I first joined a Company, I would take the time to produce a strategy document. Not only did this act as a blueprint and reference for the future, but preparing it was a great way to get up to speed on the existing situation. It enabled me to assess the abilities of my staff, and gave me an insight into the prevailing attitudes of the senior management. Inevitably, my initial impressions and opinions were eventually proved to be essentially correct, when reviewed one or two years later.

I am not the only one to find this to be the case. A number of people who give out business advice for a living, say that first impressions are invariably correct.

Lots of people better qualified than I have written books galore on how to construct a marketing strategy, and so I will simply tell you how I went about it, and let you be the judge of its relevance to your situation.

The key benefits of carrying out this task when first joining an organisation are that a) you are not yet involved in the day to day activities, b) you approach everything with an open mind, and c) no one expects you to know a great deal about what is going on. Also, as the new kid on the block, you are seen by most of your new colleagues as a potential ally, and treated accordingly. Once your feet are under the table, and you have stated your opinions, that situation no longer exists, so take full advantage while you can of the opportunity to harvest all and every opinion anyone has to offer on every subject.

In some quarters there may be resentment at your appointment. If that attitude exists, it usually becomes obvious when you sit down to talk to people, and your strategic marketing review is a great opportunity to build bridges. Occasionally, no matter how hard you try, individuals will make it obvious that they are going to be a future thorn in your side. My way of dealing with that was to ignore it and hope for the best, but the sensible thing is to plan accordingly.

Another rich source of informed opinion are the existing suppliers of marketing services. In fact, if they do not have any opinions about the business, it could be worth looking to replace them, because they should have at least that level of interest.

Once you have seen everything worth seeing, and talked to everyone who may be relevant – making very sure you have not missed anyone out who is going to see it as a snub – it is time to list the key issues. I would then run the whole lot through my What is it, Who wants it, and Why should they bother, analysis (see Planning and Analysis Chapter).

At this point, a key decision is required, in terms of how far to go with the required document/presentation. Do you show examples and illustrations of what you have in mind, or restrict yourself to saying what you think the issues are. My view was always that an illustrated proposal, even one that is intended to simply promote discussion, draws in the audience more effectively than words alone. Sometimes I have been so sure of a strategic direction that my Plan included ads, POS, and even facia design visuals, all with outline costings. Also, any proposal will almost certainly need to include electronic media these days. Most of this work can be obtained from existing suppliers on a speculative basis, as they are usually anxious to make an initial impression on the new client.

As mentioned elsewhere, it is essential to include as much supporting research as possible in order to deflect opinion based criticisms.

Inevitably, your Plan will make a sizable document or electronic presentation. Keep the meat of it down to a two page or ten slide synopsis or you will lose the audience. You should also be very clear as to what you want to take away from any meeting or presentation in terms of action points. And don't ask for the World as you are unlikely to get it. Make agreeing your Plan as simple and as painless as possible. You will know from your internal discussions and the Companies existing expenditure plans, what you are likely to achieve.

Anything you can test or sample in some way in order to prove a point is always worth doing.

However, there is sometimes a real need for radical action, and that can mean putting your neck on the block.

There is no better time to get something radical agreed than at the start of your tenure. Just make sure you get it right.

# CHAPTER 3

## Marketing Communication

"Our primary responsibility as marketing people is to communicate our offering to the target market in the most appropriate and cost effective way."

# Marketing Communication

In marketing, we pay for the *opportunity* to communicate, not the *right*. This is why the way we present, illustrate, and write our marketing message is so important.

The golden rules of effective communication apply to every kind of marketing medium, even electronic, and we break them at our peril.

With so many competing sales messages vying for the attention of potential customers, we have only seconds to ensure that ours is the one that makes them want to read on.

Once we have their attention, we must then communicate the offer in the clearest possible way. There are people who will say "if you don't tell you can't sell" and use it as an excuse to produce reams of waffling copy. In fact, it takes as few words as are needed to make the offer attractive, no more or less. Good advertising copywriters have long known the value of brevity, but many people, particularly those who build web sites, have yet to work it out. Whether copy is for an ad, mail shot or web page, it should be clear and to the point.

Also, the use of sans serif type-faces in ads and on the web may be good for aesthetics, but they are bad for readability. Otherwise, that book you are enjoying at the moment would be printed in a sans serif type face.

Also, a 22 year old designer with 20/20 vision must always remember that 8pt type is not easily read by anyone over 50. The number of times I see an unreadable business card, for example, often makes me wonder if even the person handing it out can read it themselves.

During a time in my career when I spent fortunes on TV advertising, I had dinner one evening in Monaco (not relevant, but you must admit its impressive) with Dave Trott, a top creative director. He summed up effective TV advertising communication by using six pieces of paper to represent the ads in a commercial break. On five of these, he drew a variation of a circle. Some were slightly misshaped, but all were recognisably circles. On the sixth, he drew a square. The one that stood out was, of course, the square, because it was different. He was right – that difference gets attention, which is the first objective. However, you must then communicate a sales message.

People like creative guru David Abbott, with the skills to both sell and entertain in a short TV ad, always have my profound respect. Unfortunately, there are few people who can do both, most of us having to make do with the former. The big mistake is to make do with the latter!

What amazes me is that so many TV advertisers are happy to pay vast sums of money just to entertain the viewer, and seem not to worry about actually communicating a message. This can sometimes be justified when being used as an image or awareness builder, but deep pockets are required. When Hutchinson launched Orange, they did so with the most expensive teaser campaign the UK had ever seen, involving TV ads showing a baby swimming underwater. Although they could afford it, I question the sense in creating such a high level of expectation because, when it turned out to be yet another mobile phone service, it was always going to be an anti-climax.

Perhaps because I flirted with a career in the entertainment industry, I have always recognised the power of music in communication and wondered why so many TV advertisers either ignore it, or get it wrong. Jingles can make a sales message memorable, and just using the right tune can make a powerful statement about a Company.

This also applies to radio advertising, perhaps more so.

An even more exciting use of radio is to turn its lack of visual content into a benefit by painting pictures in sound. Whereas a TV commercial shot on a palm fringed beach would cost a fortune, a radio commercial in the same location can be created by a few sound effects.

Effectively communicating a price offering can be a challenge. In TV ads, the easy way is to have a presenter scream the offer at the camera. Plenty of creative expertise has been tasked with trying to find more attractive ways to put across a value message, but few have achieved it, and many would argue that it can be a waste of time trying.

Consumer durables, for example, are bought infrequently, and the only time anyone notices such advertised offers is when they are in the market to buy. The ads will therefore attract their attention.

Also, because most potential 'big ticket' purchasers were not in the market last week, the advertiser need not worry too much about repetition. 50% off something someone wants to buy gets noticed. The same offer made when they are not in the market, does not.

Durable goods retailers also waste a lot of money trying to animate inanimate objects in TV ads. In the 70's, I devised a way of using rostrum camera techniques to produce TV ads for furniture. That involved moving the camera around a still shot of the product, rather than the product itself. Which makes sense if the product does not move, like furniture and carpets. At a time when all 'live action' commercials were shot on 35mm film involving a full crew and a chuck wagon, using stills brought the cost of TV advertising production within the reach of many Companies who would otherwise have had to choose between a 10 second slide/voice – over, or nothing.

It is also worth remembering that customer price perceptions of durable goods are usually five years out of date, and so the price points used in advertising should reflect that and be less than the current average sale value, so as not to appear expensive. It then falls to the sales staff to trade up the customer, for which those sales staff need to use price point merchandising. This means that if, for example, the advertised price is £499, similar, but better quality items should be readily available at £599, £699, and £799.

In food retailing, there is one price - point ad that everyone admires - Asda Price. This was originally created by JWT Manchester. They lost the account in the 80's, and, unbelievably, the slogan was then dropped by the Company. ASDA soon began loosing their way, and I wrote a piece for a marketing magazine suggesting that it was for two reasons. The first, dropping a slogan that was the envy of every retailer, and the second, expanding South with bigger and better units, while ignoring their aging stores in the North, so allowing Tesco and Sainsbury's in the back door.

The then Chairman, Archie Norman took notice, corrected both mistakes and was feted as a genius, so the next time he had a meal booked at our local pub, I left a message to say he owed me a drink. Needless to say, I didn't get one, and so I will not rush to tell him what to do with ITV.

In a highly competitive market, it is dangerous to be arrogant, and that's what Sainsbury's have been guilty of in the past. I remember reading an article by their Marketing Director in which he branded people who shop around as 'promiscuous customers'! Not someone from whom to take lessons in communication.

I have never been particularly good at verbal communication, and I cannot recommend many techniques which compensate for that shortcoming, other than leading by example.

I had realised early in my career that my ability to convince colleagues on a Board of Directors that my radical answers were the way to go, was sadly ineffective. A well researched and weighty proposal document did sometimes provide good support but was not, in itself, adequate. An entertaining presentation often helped, but only when it could be made to be completely relevant.

The way I have had to do it can best be described as the 'cock on the block' method. This involves either getting on with it, or sampling it to an extent that proves the point. When I wanted William Hill to act upon the radical recommendations of a shop designer, for example, we had to refit a large shop on a major High Street to demonstrate the concept, and the technology. This opened on the first day of the Cheltenham Festival with a

BBC outside broadcast unit showing live pictures from it, and it changed the face of betting shops for ever, as I knew it would.

However, to make this method work, you must be 100% certain that you are right!

Although I cover advertising and the internet elsewhere, it is worth pointing out that the golden rules of communication also apply to them. There is so little time in which to grab the attention of your potential customer that your sales message must be clear and to the point.

I realise that this Chapter wanders across a number of marketing disciplines and my experiences, but I strongly believe we should always remember that *our primary responsibility as marketing people is to communicate our offering to the target market in the most appropriate and cost effective way.* Sometimes it matters less that it looks good, just so long as it works.

# CHAPTER 4

## Marketing economics

"WHEN THE BELL RINGS, I WANT YOU TO COME OUT DISCUSSING RECENT THEORETICAL EMPIRICAL AND METHODOLOGICAL ADVANCES IN MICROECONOMICS."

"I strongly recommend that you ignore all economists, and treat the pronouncements of academics with scepticism."

# Marketing Economics

Mention economics, and up pops an economist with a 'model'. A model is a devise that can legitimatise such activities as 120% mortgages, or running up a £trillion national debt.

Fortunately, we marketing people do not need economists; most of us can work out the economics of a marketing strategy for ourselves.

Neither do we need the academic community to come up with mathematical equations designed to illustrate how much should be spent in order to achieve a given sales objective.

In fact, I strongly recommend that you ignore all economists, and treat the pronouncements of academics with scepticism. Just remember that most of them are first and foremost out to make a name for themselves.

Any discussion about marketing economics should revolve around the cost of marketing something, no more or less.

The levels of marketing expenditure required to do any marketing job will depend on many different factors, but the first task is get a clear idea of the job it will be required to do.

Once that expectation is understood, it is important to ensure you are convinced that the 'product' matches the objective.

When satisfied with the product, and the size and scale of the objective is clear, it is time to look around.

The target market is the first thing to consider. You need to be clear on who they are and where they are.

Somehow, you also have to ensure that the target market is going to be receptive to the product. For a few ideas on how to do that, look elsewhere in this book.

Almost always, there will be competitors in the way of the objective, and so it is important to analyse their activities, particularly their market share and marketing spend.

Then, and only then, can you begin to plan the marketing activity you believe will be needed for the task – creative work, media, print, internet etc – which in turn will indicate the required expenditure.

Occasionally, you will find that the money required to fund your ideal campaign cannot be justified by the projected sales. You must therefore either trim the expenditure, or increase the sales forecast. This is probably the hardest part of a marketing director's job, and many a faint heart will try to run away from the responsibility. The only way to avoid the decision but still save face, is to decide that the desired expenditure level will be a gamble that requires some collective responsibility, and that will usually mean a Board decision. However, such a cop out will not go unnoticed, and you can bet that your pitch to the Board will only result in a positive outcome if the CEO decides to back it. Even then, if it all goes belly up, you will take the blame.

Therefore, if it is possible to make an expenditure decision without exceeding your authority, always do so. If you frequently get things wrong, you could find yourself out of a job, but get things wrong frequently and you are probably in the wrong job anyway.

Monitoring the results from your marketing spend is just as important as getting the spend right, particularly if you have stuck your neck out. In some businesses, that is easier said than done. Often in durable goods retailing, for example, the promoted items are loss leaders, designed to get people into the stores so that they can be 'sold up'. It is, therefore, the effect on the overall turnover that indicates success or failure. Even that can be affected by external influences such as weather, for example. In that type of business, the quickest way to find out what the marketing has done for turnover is to organise feedback from the sales staff. On one occasion, I had a problem with 'product shock'. The promoted items looked considerably better in the advertising than they did in reality, and people responding to the ads were resisting attempts to sell them up. Fortunately, the shop staff gave me the 'heads up' because without it, I would not have realised what was happening. I had gone too far, and it was a lesson learned.

So what are the basic economics of marketing? Essentially, it is the cost of the activity required to bring something to the market, by which I mean a sale. The manufacturing, or cost to buy, of the product tends to be largely outside the control of most marketing departments, as are expenses such as occupation costs. So, concentrate on those factors over which you have a direct control.

You should always consider the *overall* costs when assessing expenditure.

Marketing staff for example, can represent a massive on-cost, which may be better spent on other things. At one time, BT had some big marketing departments, many of which had little or no budget for media expenditure, or any other above the line marketing activity. I always thought that they should have employed less people, but given them some money to spend.

In retailing, the cost of things such as external signage, displays, samples, and discounted margins must be seen as marketing expenditure, and as such must be controlled by, and the responsibility of, the marketing department.

So when allocating and monitoring expenditure to products or projects, make sure you apply all of the costs, and look out for any that you should have control over, but don't.

In the end, it comes down to bottom line, or net profit, but that profit may not come immediately, because marketing can be an investment. Just make sure everyone understands that is your intention.

I apologise if some of the above is a little simplistic, but marketing economics is always a question of getting the basics right, so that you know exactly how much it is costing to market something. The makeup of that will vary from industry to industry, and sometimes from Company to Company within the same industry, so I have resisted the temptation to throw in a few of my own little tools, as you need to find the system that best suits you and yours.

Above all, ignore the preaching's of those who try to make everything ten times more complicated than they really are, such as a Paper I read recently which had been produced by three international business schools, entitled *Economics for marketing revisited*, and which set out to provide evidence supporting the statement that 'recent theoretical, empirical, and methodological advances in microeconomics are decisive to the progress of marketing science', blaming 'irreconcilable differences between economists and psychologists' for the lack of knowledge dissemination.

Just let them get on with it, I say.

# CHAPTER 5

## Advertising

"I considered waiting for an advertising agency to do everything for me to be lazy and stressful."

# Advertising

I have read lots of the books written about advertising, but only one impressed me. It is called Scientific Advertising by Claude Hopkins, and I recommend that you read it.

In order to give a flavour, I have included the Chapter on Headlines as an addendum.

Most of it is as relevant now as it was when Hopkins wrote it in 1923, and as it is only 100 pages, we can assume that the attention span of the average marketing person was then what it is now, so he kept it brief, as have I.

Not that I agree with everything he says, but I make allowances, knowing that he was a copywriter by trade. Some of his tips on how to construct an advertisement are right on the button. 'Don't think of people in the mass' he says when talking about how to write an ad, 'think of a typical individual'.

For anyone who is not familiar with Hopkins, he was an advertising copywriter who enjoyed a salary of $185,000 a year – in 1907!

Advertising presentation is far from simple, but it is relatively straightforward. Keep the message brief and to the point, and address it in a way that will attract the people you wish to target. An ad should always build aspiration. That can often be achieved simply by ensuring that the product looks its best, something that is often ignored for 'creative' reasons.

In fact, the most difficult aspect of ad production for the average marketer is coping with the egos' of the creative people who design and write most good advertising. When they come up with something wonderful, they are easy to deal with. But a lot of the time its either workmanlike, which is OK, or it is rubbish, in which case you have to find a way to send them back to the drawing board without being buried in teddy bears flying out of cots. And God help the ad agency account man or client who suggests an alternative idea! Even the best creative departments in the world, and we have any number in the UK, produce utter dross at times, but try telling them that. Not that you can rely on me to provide you with the answer, because I never found it. I remember Peter Mead of Abbott Mead Vickers, or AMV as it is now, telling me how pleased he was that he had acquired some brownie points with the creative department that morning, which made me relieved to discover that I was not the only one to have a problem with the jeans and T-shirt brigade. Even those of us who started our working life in the creative business, lose all credibility with that department as soon as we don a suit.

However, I do not underestimate the value of creativity, and once when trying to turn around an ad agency, and faced with a need for a top creative director, I reduced my own salary by a third so I could afford to recruit one.

Although creativity is the most demanding, the most complex part of any ad campaign is, in my opinion, choosing the correct vehicle to carry the message. Media selection has become more complicated as the media has fragmented. The plethora of TV channels, and the rise of the internet, has changed things out of all recognition to even 10 years ago. Major advertisers can no longer rely only on the mainstream national press titles and TV channels when they wish to mass communicate. On the other hand, advertisers with smaller budgets can now more easily target discreet consumer groups by selectively choosing the most appropriate media.

As a marketing director I was at times heavily involved in managing big TV media spends. We would choose the programmes in which to advertise at the start of each 'season' based on previews shown to us as major advertisers. This usually worked well, but one year I committed a big spend to a new drama series which was to be shown at 9pm on Friday evenings, a key time to advertise consumer durables. In those days, TV viewing figures, or ratings, were not available until two weeks after transmission, but I did not have to wait for the ratings to know that I had backed a loser. It was a disaster, and when they were eventually published, the ratings showed that ITV's Friday night audience levels had plummeted. The then 'godfather' of TV advertising was a chap called Ron Miller, the sales director of LWT, at the time when Greg

Dyke was its COE. I phoned Ron to find out if anything could be done, and to pull our expenditure if it couldn't. The result was that the series moved to a late night slot in favour of repeats of a popular show which promptly doubled the ratings. No one even missed the original programme; it really was so bad.

It was the only occasion I know of, when advertiser pressure actually changed an ITV schedule. It also shows that good quality repeats can be more effective than dross.

Because there are now so many TV channels, much of the airtime is sold as a package, often linked to achieving a set number of ratings. This is fine up to a point, but it's a lazy media buyer that buys a whole campaign on that basis, and it's a lazy client that allows it. When Channel 4 launched, I approved a ratings deal that eventually needed 300 spots to fulfil the agreement. That sounds good but it simply meant that we bored the same few people over and over and over again. It's important to look past ratings and take a considered view on the audience figures, in terms of the people you think you are getting to from the programming in which the ads are appearing, then fine tune as needed to aim for the audience you want. There is often a geodemographic analysis of major media coverage to help with targeting, but be careful.

I was heavily involved in the early days of ACORN - a classification of residential neighbourhoods - which is based on census data. It can be an extremely useful tool with which to compare the profile of the desired audience to that achieved, but needs a large sample size to be really conclusive. However, such techniques are constantly evolving, and so I would simply advocate that everyone involved in buying media should assess the value of these systems for themselves.

It is worth remembering that, although 'fixing' spots is an expensive business, a little lobbying in the right places can often get spots 'placed' where you want them to be, even local rate spots. Very few advertisers pay to 'fix' spots, so there is a lot of discretion available, and building a relationship with a few people at the Station can make sure you get your share.

As I write, the rules on product placement are being relaxed, opening up a whole new opportunity for negotiation.

I was lucky enough to catch the end of the great days of the National Press in the 60's when Fleet Street advertising departments were full of wonderful characters. As a young man with a lot of money to spend on national press space, these people made time for me, and I learned an enormous amount from them, while having a lot of fun in the process. Slowly they disappeared with the advent of Messrs Murdoch and Matthews, and a new breed of hard talking media people emerged. Strangely, it was easier to negotiate a good deal with the hard cases, because it became a more professional process. The downside was that everything had to be negotiated – position, copy changes etc – which the old timers would throw in for free for someone they liked.

If cultivating good relations with TV execs was important, establishing a relationship with the key press people was absolutely essential.

Unlike the more aloof TV top brass, many of the press barons were very accessible, even those who were considered to be giants. Robert Maxwell was a case in point. I remember when I was at William Hill, joining him for dinner in his office, and to watch Liverpool playing in a European Cup final.

Tragically, it was the night of the Heysel Stadium disaster, and as it started to unfold, Bob excused himself to go and hassle his editor. However, before he left he reminded me that he had won a large bet on his team Oxford United achieving promotion 3 seasons in succession. He then asked me to check on a second bet he was certain he had also placed with us on the same subject.

Now these bets were enormous, and Maxwell was not a mug punter – he bet wisely, and he bet well. It could have turned into an evening marked not only by the dreadful events in Brussels, but also a large financial loss. However, to my relief, the following day I discovered that Maxwell had placed his second bet with Ladbrokes.

Later that same evening, by which time I certainly was somewhat the worse for wear, Maxwell reappeared with his editor in tow, and sat us around a table to discuss what he should say about the evening's tragedy when he appeared on breakfast TV the following morning. Needless to say, the famous boxing promoter, the football manager, the two chairmen of major sporting institutions, and yours truly, did not help Robert Maxwell find the answer to football hooliganism. The discussion was later written up by Private Eye as a 'meeting of sporting luminaries' and we were supposed to have quaffed champagne and dined on lobster as we watched the tragedy. In fact we watched in horror and ate little, which was why I felt the effects of a few glasses of wine, not champagne.

It never pays to rub someone's nose in it, however desperate they are to do a deal, because in advertising, you can never tell where people are going to work next, and the boot could easily be on the other foot the next time you meet.

My predecessor at Allied Carpets had moved on to become our CEO, but would keep putting his nose into the bigger media negotiations. Until, that is, we met a major TV contractor to set up a new 12 month deal. The guy negotiating on behalf of the TV station had previously worked for our ad agency as a media buyer, and our man had made his life a misery. It became very clear very quickly that he was going to get his own back, and he started by stating that our rates would be revised upwards by 50%!

When negotiating any media deal, it is worth listing the points for discussion in advance and deciding what you want, and what you will settle for. Sometimes, you do not seem to have a good argument or alternative media that can be used as a bartering tool, but in fact, you always have something. For example, a national chain opening a retail outlet in a town that falls into a TV region where they do not already have branches, will need local ad rates to make TV advertising viable. But, the TV station will say, it is not a local business and therefore does not qualify. I had this problem on many occasions as we rolled out Allied Carpets, but I would argue that consumers use a local outlet and it matters not one jot to them that the Company have a wonderful shop in London, or hundreds of stores elsewhere, because consumers see a retail Company as the local outlet(s). If that approach didn't work I would revert to writing the TV budget down on a piece of paper alongside two pre-prepared media schedules, one with them getting the TV spend using local spots, one using the same money in alternative media, local press, radio etc. It never failed to get the deal, and once the precedence is set, a lot of additional stores can be added to that Region before anyone questions the rate again

Why pay a dog and bark yourself, you may ask. Well, I considered waiting for an ad agency to do everything for me to be lazy, and stressful. At Allied Carpets I could point to MEAL expenditure statistics that showed us spending double our actual figure, indicating an overall 50% saving on rate card, and that the same statistics showed our sister Company Asda, who used the same ad agency, were achieving only a 30% saving – and their actual spend was double ours. That was achieved by getting actively involved, not sitting back and waiting for the Agency.

When I moved to William Hill from Allied Carpets, their National Press spend was tiny in comparison with Allied, yet I immediately negotiated a 30% overall discount, which effectively meant that it never cost Hills a penny to employ me. I was able to do this because the National Press sales directors were so used to me demanding discounts that, when I asked, they just handed them over.

To get back to the creative function, I do not see why a marketing director, or agency account director, with a good idea, should feel it necessary to 'sell' that idea to the ad agency creative department. The best work I have ever produced personally was as a client, using a small agency that let me get on with it. The Company I worked for at the time had 30 enormous furniture stores throughout the UK, trading under 15 different names. This had come about through acquiring various family businesses, and leaving them to trade under the family name, often with a family member in charge. Each Monday morning I would decide which stores to advertise on the coming Friday, and what to feature in the ads. The agency had then to produce anything up to 20 different ads, design the point of sale materials, and book the press space. Our printers also had to produce and distribute the supporting point of sale materials, often in a three day time frame.

Everyone was so busy that I could get on with other things without having to worry about bruising any egos.

I had quickly realised that the advantage of having all the individual businesses was that we would easily qualify for the very lowest local TV rates. The problem was how to produce decent commercials with limited resources, bearing in mind that video was in its infancy and never used outside a TV studio. As the Agency had enough on its plate, I set about solving the problem myself.

I had noticed a Stork margarine commercial on air, with a centre section comprised of still photographs animated by moving the camera around. I called the Agency involved, and they were kind enough to send me a print of the commercial. I then called up one of the fashion photographers that I had used at John Collier, and we went off to one of our stores and took lots of shots of furniture, including things like a swivel chair in six different positions. The Stork Agency had told me that I would need to find a film production house with a good rostrum camera man, and that is what I did. The result was fabulous.

Instead of a voice over, I asked my former rock band colleagues, who had their own recording studio, to write a jingle, and that also worked well.

The idea caught on, and a small industry grew up around rostrum camera commercials.

Some of our stores were in outposts of the ITV empire, such as Border and Westward. Not only did that keep airtime costs down, but the Stations were very accommodating, offering studios, editing, and in one case, a loan of the OB unit to make live action commercials in-store.

I must say that having a top ad agency, and top creative talent working on your business, is a privilege. The trouble is that they often refuse to accept criticism even when their work is not good enough.

Indeed, every young person joining a creative department seems to become instantly arrogant.

I accept that ideas are subjective, but someone has to make a judgement, and if I had to carry the can, I made the decisions. Although I would always bow to the knowledge and expertise of the great creative directors, any jumped up copywriter or visualiser that gave me the 'take it or leave it' line, soon got a flea in his or her ear.

The media department, on the other hand, welcome a client involvement, yet are often ignored. I always enjoyed spending time with agency media buyers, and found the whole process stimulating.

Finally, lets remember that we pay for an *opportunity* to communicate, not the *right.*

In creative terms, that means we must always make it easy for the reader, viewer, or listener, to understand what it is that we are trying to sell.

# CHAPTER 6

## Choosing an advertising agency

BEWARE OF A SLICK PITCH TEAM
BEARING GIFTS.

"Remember that lunch they bought? Well, it is probably on your job bag, marked up 20%, waiting to be charged out to you."

# Choosing an Advertising Agency

I have been responsible for choosing an ad agency on a number of occasions, most notably for John Collier, Allied Carpets and William Hill. I have also pitched for some major clients while running two full service agencies.

The first time I had to go through the process of picking an agency was in the 60's, when I was only 21 years old. We were a big advertiser, and so in the course of selection I got to meet some of the countries leading ad people, and some of the sharks. One guy sent his Jaguar S Type to collect me, asked me if I liked it, and told me that if he got the account, he would take my Ford Corsair GT, and replace it with the Jaguar. He didn't tell me how he thought I would explain that to our transport manager, and I didn't ask. Another told me that my personal 'commission' would be paid in cash.

Generally speaking, there are 4 key factors in choosing an agency.

You must get along with the personnel involved, and so you must ensure that the people doing the pitch are the same people who will run the account if they are successful. It's no good warming to the Chairman if you will only see him at the annual review, or the creative genius if he is the guy used only for pitches, and who will be handing you over to some spotty youth with an ego the size of Richard Branson.

They must show understanding of the market, and your products.

The creative work should be practical *and* should turn you on.

They must be capable of spending your money effectively, and their own charges should be reasonable.

I was a Production Manager of an advertising agency at age 18, so I knew what production costs should be and what to look out for. You must expect, for example, the cost of pitching to you to be sat on what is known as a suspense account bag. All jobs, including pitches, progressing through an agency have a numbered 'job bag', or the electronic equivalent on which the various charges are noted, and into which go copies of everything produced. When the bag is 'closed' the job is charged. If appointed, the Account Director responsible for your pitch will attempt to claw back the charges on the suspense account job bag, by feeding the costs onto chargeable jobs, over a period of a year.

It is better to demand that you see the suspense account at the outset, and agree a figure to pay it off. But beware – there will be a lot of costs on there that they will not want you to see. Remember that lunch they bought? Well, it could be on your job bag, marked up 20% to be charged out to you.

In fact, it is worth remembering that any lunch the agency buy will end up on your job bags. Aware of this, I would usually pay for lunch. However, I know one client MD who would pay for lunch and give the receipt to the account man so he could claim it back on expenses, thinking he was doing him a favour. The account man did claim it back, and then he put the charge on the same client's job bag, where it was marked up 20% and charged back to him. I discovered this when taking over that agency as MD, and knowing that the client did it, because he had told me so.

We acquired a new client once because he had disputed a charge made by his previous agency, which, he was told, had then been written off, only for it to arrive back on his desk with the next batch of invoices, marked in the account director's handwriting, 'charge to any of this client's current job bags'.

Ad men are not Bankers. Only a very few earn Bankers wages, but they are well paid, which makes running an agency an expensive business. If you screw too tight a deal out of an agency, you will get what you are paying for in terms of personnel, and could end up in a permanent battle with your account man as he tries desperately to make money out of you. Once again, it is better for both parties to be up front, and discuss charges openly.

If you have a big media spend, you may appoint an agency, and a media buying shop. Whereas in the past, an agency would make 15% commission on your media spend, which often went to subsidise production costs, splitting the creative/production and media functions has saved major advertisers a fortune in commission payments, but has meant that the agencies have had to start charging realistic rates for creative and production work.

It has also meant that most of the smaller agencies offer services spanning marketing, sales promotion, and direct marketing as well as advertising. This makes agency selection a complex operation, and it is essential to have a look at what they have done in the past, and speak to people who should know how good they are at spending money, media sales execs, for example..

Some smaller advertisers prefer to buy services from a whole raft of specialist service providers such as design studios, PR consultants, web designers, etc. This is fine so long as the marketing manager/director knows what he is doing, as he needs to be very hands on. My view is that, even after all I have said elsewhere, a good agency relationship is worth paying for. Your suppliers of marketing services need to know your business if they are going to make a serious contribution and not going to take up a lot of your time, which would be better spent on planning and strategy. Someone you only use on an occasional basis would find it difficult to justify the time it takes to do that.

I am not for throwing money away, but creative services cannot be bought like cans of beans, and the current trend for smaller client companies to expect their marketing people to produce creative work on a computer, is a joke.

I also think that the standard of web related presentation is dire, and the sooner web designers learn to apply basic design principals to internet sites, the better.

Until they do, your ad agency, even if they do not offer internet design services, can give you access to designers and typographers who you can use to vet the design of your internet material.

Just remember that an ad agency is a business, just like yours, and in return for providing you with advertising and services that make profits for you, has to make profits for itself.

# CHAPTER 7

## Merchandising

"Giving the design team some actual customer data, rather than management opinion, allows them to formulate their own views, based on their interpretation of the findings."

# Merchandising

I walked into our Middlesbrough store one day in 1972, to see a 3 piece suite front and centre in the doorway with three different prices on it. The swing ticket had one price, a standard show card another, and a larger special offer card carried a third. "Do you not think Clive", I said to the Manager, "That three different prices could confuse people?" "Not really", he said, "Some people want to pay more than others".

Clive had a point, - although he was going about it in a way guaranteed to cause some excitement in the Trading Standards Office.

Pricing is an art form in certain retail situations, particularly when there are few major brands, as in furniture. Asking too little for a furnishing item can lead prospective purchasers to assume that it must be poor quality. There are, in fact, few reasons for keeping margins slim in that business, particularly if an item is in an exclusive cover or design that defies comparison elsewhere. Obviously, it is important to have some products in each category priced keenly in order to get people through the door, but sometimes the ranges on offer at higher price points have cost the retailer very little more than the 'loss leaders'.

If that sounds like a consumer rip off, let me hasten to point out that big gross profit margins are essential in furniture retailing, because the stock turn is low, the occupation costs are high, and the handling problems lead to lots of markdowns due to damages and the soiling of display items.

Pricing is but one aspect of merchandising, although it is a key factor, particularly on branded FMCG items. Display, or making goods look or sound attractive, is very important for some merchandise, and extremely important for fashion and style items. In some ways, it is a shame that so much retailing now takes place in sheds, because many have no windows in which to display goods in order to show them at their best.

I always say that good retail merchandising starts on the inside and works outwards. Get the staff right, then the product range, design the display area to compliment the merchandise, use stylish graphics and point of sale material to provide emphasis, and then attend to the outside. That means designing signage and widow areas to reflect the required image. Obviously, having a store design framework in place is essential to much of this.

I was lucky enough to work with some great shop designers. All of the retail Companies I was involved with got a benefit from innovative design work, even William Hill. I was looking for a design House when at Hills, and one of the Companies in the frame decided to take a trip around some of our shops. At the first outlet they went into, one of them asked the nice lady cashier behind the bandit screen how to put on a bet. "Young man", she said, "If you don't already, you should not start gambling!"

My favourite designer story involves a furniture industry conference on Jersey in 1975.

I had been asked to chair one of the sessions, but to my disappointment, I was allocated a discussion on trade unions, rather than the one on store design. That did, however, prove to be fortunate because the top designer chosen to do the presentation decided his first slide would be the Nazi flag – a swastika on a red background. "Ladies and gentlemen," he starts, "this is the greatest corporate identity ever devised", at which point half his, largely Jewish, audience stood up and left in disgust.

Not for the first time, I realised that creative people need guidance, and so I tried to ensure that shop designers working for me always had a good brief. The best way to do this, I found, was to commission some attitudinal consumer research using group discussions. Giving the design team some actual customer data, rather than management opinion, allowed them to formulate their own views based on their interpretation of the findings.

One furniture chain I worked for had an innovative approach to window merchandising. In addition to enhancing inexpensive furniture with expensive pictures and bric-a-brac, they would have a visual joke, leaving a riding crop on a bed, or a saucy novel on a bedside table open at an interesting page. It was the sexy seventies, and so no one complained.

As Advertising Manager of John Collier in the 60's, I had some input into window displays, and suggested that the new plastic grass which had recently been launched by Cyril Lord Carpets (long before Astroturf) would look good in our sportswear window displays. We had 100's of shops, so it was a big order for Cyril Lord, who thanked our Boss by fitting the same grass carpet around his outdoor pool. Some weeks later, the Chairman asked me if I had checked the sportswear windows recently. As I had not, I took myself down to our nearest shop, where I got a shock. The 'grass' had turned blue. It had turned out to be light sensitive.

Graphic design becomes very important when considering POS materials. In supermarketing, it is important to functionally signpost the whereabouts of goods, as well as drawing attention to offers, so as to provide customers with a means of completing their shop in the minimum amount of time, and giving them the satisfaction of finding a bargain or two.

In durable goods retailing, the materials can provide information, flag up offers, or simply add colour and style to the displays. The latter is of particular importance in fashion and clothing retailing. Amazingly, Marks and Spencer ignored the benefits of POS material for many years, as they did advertising. I remember attending a retail marketing conference chaired by Harry Sheppard, the M&S advertising manager, in the days when M&S never advertised. At one point, Harry was down to do a presentation about M&S, and I couldn't wait to see what he would do. Somehow, he managed to fill a full half hour explaining the process involved in putting a 6" X 2" show card with 'REDUCED' in white out of a red background, on just one hanging fixture in each store. In M&S terms, this was the cutting edge of retail marketing. Harry was a nice man, and became Chairman of the Oxford Street Traders Association in later life, but I did wonder how he passed his time at M&S.

Merchandising programmes are often planned on an annual basis. In fact, the seasons are key factors. Unfortunately, Sales, which were traditionally confined to January and August, are now spread throughout the year and introduced whenever a retailer needs a boost. In doing so, Sales have lost their impact. Why some retailers do not have a little more imagination and use 'events' to achieve the same thing, is a mystery to me. When at Allied Carpets, we were constantly discounting, but at least we tried to put a different spin on the promotions. I confess that we were perceived as having a lot of Sales. I once agreed that Allied would part sponsor a West End musical about an Advertising Agency. We were to be depicted as a client, together with Babycham, General Motors, and LBC. Although it cost relatively little, and we got a lot of publicity out of it, it was awful and only ran for a few weeks. However, one thing did make me laugh. A scene showed a meeting at the Agency, when one character said, "I think we should suggest to Allied that their Sale has been running a little too long". "Oh, how long?", said another. "Fifteen years", came the reply.

# CHAPTER 8

## Planning and analysis techniques

SOME OF THE MARKETING TECHNIQUES TAUGHT BY
LEARNED PROFESSORS SEEM DESIGNED MORE TO MAKE
THE 'PROF' LOOK CLEVER, THAN AS A GENUINE
MARKETING TOOL.

"Usually, the CEO knows which strategic direction the Company is heading in, but has omitted to tell anyone else."

# Planning and Analysis

I realised many years ago that some of the marketing development techniques taught by learned professors on business courses are designed more to make 'prof' look clever than as a genuine marketing tool.

There are books galore on this subject, mostly by the same learned professors, all advocating that authors pet theory.

I will therefore restrict my recommendations to the following, as the only ones I ever use, and can recommend, which you may not already be aware of.

Interestingly, the first came from an ad agency creative director called Chris Sharpe, who used it to plan advertising campaigns in the days when he, Bernstein, Abbott, and other British creative talent, produced the worlds best advertising.

It involves pulling together the relevant people within the Company, and asking three questions:

What is it?

Who wants it?

Why should they bother?

This clarifies the service or product offering, identifies the target market, and provides a list of benefits, which should be ranked in order of importance.

It always helps to point the way forward, and can serve to highlight any shortcomings that need to be addressed.

The above aids development, but occasionally it is worth carrying out a review. For this, I use something I call:

The Good

The Bad

The Ugly

This simply involves listing all your recent initiatives under each heading, so that in future you look for more of the first, less of the second, and none of the third.

I have seen some absolute nonsense on this subject, taught by people who purport to be business advisors. Generally, the only people worth listening too are those who have been there, and done it themselves – with one exception. I did attend a Harvard Business Summer School, where actual case histories are used to teach business planning and strategy. A career enhancing experience, and one that I can recommend.

All marketing planning has to fall in line with Company strategy, but it is amazing how often the process throws up a lack of strategic direction in the Company, and prompts the need to produce one. However, do be careful who you discuss this with, and how you broach the subject. Usually, the CEO knows exactly which strategic direction the Company is heading in, but has omitted to tell anyone else!

Finally, anyone who doubts the value of planning need look no further than our current Government. Would you invade a country without first deciding what you would do with it afterwards, or buy a Bank without setting a remuneration policy? Still, we are just marketing people, what do we know?

# CHAPTER 9

## Marketing in a Recession

THE LAST TIME THE ECONOMY WAS IN ANYTHING LIKE IT'S PRESENT STATE, WE ONLY HAD POWER THREE DAYS A WEEK. AND THE REST OF THE TIME WE WERE SELLING BY TILLEY LAMP.

"Don't look for uncompetitive margins in an effort to compensate for falling sales. 100% of nothing is nothing."

# Marketing in a Recession

As I write this, the storm clouds are gathering, and without wishing to get too Churchillion, we may be moving into a battle for financial survival.

Before you, with the benefit of hindsight, tell me that was an exaggeration, let me tell you that the thing to do in any downturn/crisis/recession is to plan for the worst and rejoice if it turns out to be better than you thought.

Its Lord Hanson's golden rule – if you can live with the worst possible downside, get on with it. So whatever your plans involve, be sure you can survive if they don't work.

Let us assume that you are reading this in 2010, and unemployment has hit 3 million. The debt fuelled bubble has burst all over the UK economy, and we are all up to our necks in it. What should you have done and what can you do?

For this exercise, I will assume that you are a fully grown businessperson first, and a marketer second.

Unlike the lunatics that ran our economy in the 10 years prior to 2009, you would not seek to increase your indebtedness, but you must make sure that you have a big enough facility to provide the working capital to see your plans through.

As money dries up, in most industries cash is king, so look after what you have, and don't allow your customers too much unsecured credit.

Don't look for uncompetitive margins in an effort to compensate for falling sales. 100% of nothing is nothing.

Eliminate all unnecessary, and unplanned, expenditure.

Get rid of unnecessary personnel, including those lame ducks you have put up with for years. Its tough, but you must put the interests of the majority first.

Re-examine every capital project in relation to the plan and question all capital expenditure (even if it has done 50,000 miles!).

Set realistic goals, and use only closely targeted and cost effective marketing techniques to achieve them. It's not a time to image build, or fly kites.

The last is the most important by far. You can reduce costs all you like, but without *turnover*, it becomes a meaningless exercise. The trick is to pick those sales opportunities that suit the times.

Other considerations also take effect in a recession.

Customer A could potentially buy more than customer B, but is A more likely to become a bad debt?

Are the sales people targeted in a way which ensures that they do not put dodgy business on the books to earn a bonus (now called banker business)? My view of bonuses is and always will be that they should only be used as a means of rewarding exceptional results, not for achieving targets. I only once agreed to work for a bonus based on achieving a target, and I was never paid because the Company forgot to register the arrangement at the time of a government pay freeze. The group Chairman was very apologetic, and invited me to 'use' my Company Amex card, which I did with gusto – but you can't pay your mortgage with Dom Perignon champagne or Pellegrino suits.

The usual question for the marketing department when times are tough is how much can be removed from the marketing budget. Do not allow this to be viewed as a stand alone question. It is appropriate to revisit every aspect of the marketing plan and review its feasibility, but if you need to spend in order to achieve an objective, you must point out that less expenditure means less achievement and no expenditure could mean no achievement at all.

Remember that those you are selling to are probably taking the same actions as you are in order to survive. Your offers have to recognise that, and be expressed accordingly. Finding ways to get people to spend money on a purchase that could be deferred is hard at the best of times, and almost impossible in a recession, but it can be done by finding the right trigger. For example, one tactic that can work if you are marketing big ticket items to consumers and have cash reserves is to offer delayed payment terms, a la DFS. DFS Chairman Graham, the noble Lord, Kirkham has long advocated, and effectively used, this sales tactic, but I can't help but wonder how it will play in a really deep recession.

By the time you read this, we may have found out. Certainly Graham is not one to cut back on his marketing spend when things are tough, and at the time of writing the DFS TV ads are coming thick and fast.

The last time the economy was in anything like its present state, I had just taken over as Marketing Director of Scotland's largest retail furnisher. At one stage, we only had power on three days a week, and the rest of the time, we were selling by Tilley lamp. Not only did we not reduce marketing expenditure, but I also set about refurbishing the stores. It worked, and we prospered, but with the benefit of thirty years more experience than I had then, I'm not sure I would be brave enough to do it now.

Having said that, we used a very strong price proposition linked to ads which made the products look fabulous. Once we got the customer in the store, we dressed the products with outrageously expensive accessories and lighting. At a time when our competition was piling it high to sell it cheap, we made an inexpensive item look terrific, and it worked.

Whatever you do, do something, as long as it complies with that Golden Rule - if you can live with the downside, get on with it.

Then, if you got it wrong, at least you tried.

# CHAPTER 10

## Sales or marketing?

"Give everyone a simple way to evaluate a marketing idea. It can save hours of tactfully telling colleagues that their latest brainwave is absolute rubbish."

# Sales or Marketing?

Most of my marketing career was spent in retail Companies, who rarely have a 'sales' director of the type that is normally found in service or manufacturing Companies. However, when running Ad Agencies, I had many clients with both sales and marketing directors, and quite a few with someone called the Sales *and* Marketing Director. Now, I think that I am a good marketer, but freely admit to knowing absolutely nothing about sales management. In fact, I am also such a lousy salesman that I would struggle to sell a cup of water to a millionaire who was dying of thirst. My point is that I believe there is a vast difference between the skill set required to be a good sales director and that of a marketing director. Few people, in my experience, possess both.

The Agency Group I ran at one time had a marketing consultancy division. We carried out marketing assessments of many different and varied Companies on behalf of the DTI under the Enterprise Initiative Scheme. I involved myself in lots of these jobs, which included a wide range of service companies, manufacturers, and even the UK's largest distributer of wedding dresses. Usually, we were called in by the CEO because he knew he had a problem, but not what that problem was. Often, the problem turned out to be the person responsible for marketing within the organisation, who did not know what they were doing. Significantly, these people were often called the Sales and Marketing Director.

Sales Directors tend to see that title as a leg up, but who is daft enough to give them the marketing mantle without first making sure that they know something about marketing?

This could be because an attitude exists within some organisations, that marketing is little more than salesmanship in print, and so how hard can it be?

I came across the worst example of this type of arrogance at York University, who had invited our local Branch of the Chartered Institute of Marketing to an evening presentation of their plans for a commercial science village. At one point, a science professor stood up and told us that they did not intend to involve marketing professionals, as they themselves were highly intelligent people who would "simply read a few marketing books and get on with it". It sums up one of the biggest problems faced by the corporate marketing professional – just about everyone believes they are a marketing expert.

The only way to cope with this, in my opinion, is to inject an acceptable amount of discipline into the proceedings. Give colleagues a simple way to evaluate a marketing idea. It can save hours of tactfully telling them that their latest brainwave is absolute rubbish, or even more difficult, having to tell your boss that his idea, which probably came from his wife, and which he always presents to you at a Board Meeting in front of everyone, sucks.

The thing is, some of the ideas that come from non-marketing colleagues are good, and you don't want them to feel that you are not interested in anything they may suggest. So, have a simple analysis mechanism with which they can check the viability of their idea before putting it to you. This not only filters out the dross, but encourages the right kind of input. I tended to use my *what is it, who wants it, and why should they bother* checklist, because it is simple and easy to understand, but a SWOT analysis can work just as well, and has the advantage that most people are familiar with it.

Often, there is a dispute within an organisation about which comes first, sales or marketing. The marketing people will want the sales team to achieve targets set by them, and the sales department will want to set a realistic sales target around which the marketing people must construct a budget. Marketing usually wins, because it makes no sense to do things the other way around – unless, that is, there is a sales director who is called the sales and marketing director!

# CHAPTER 11

## The Internet

TAKE EVERY OPPORTUNITY TO GET THE WEB
ADDRESS OUT THERE.

"An internet site should add something positive to the business, and so the objective behind creating it must be clear."

# The Internet

Never has so much rubbish been written and spoken on one subject. I don't pretend to be an expert on internet marketing, but I do know that the myths surrounding the internet are largely bunkum, and that, at least in terms of objectives and presentation; it should be treated as just another marketing and communication medium.

These days everyone in business should consider having a web site because it is now probably the single most important means of commercial communication. More importantly, everyone in business can now afford a web site.

It was not ever thus. In 1996, our PLC had been quoted on the London Stock Exchange for less than a year when my partner decided that we must have a web site for our soccer information product called Teamtalk, which we were selling to fans by way of a premium rate telephone service. The internet site would replicate the premium rate telephone service, which provided up to the minute news about every team in the Football League, using our 20 in-house journalists to do so. The journalists must then not only record every item of news on to our telephone system, but also type it into the internet pages, which, of course, required more people. It also needed a massive internet site, which eventually cost an enormous amount of money to create. The unscheduled expenditure caused us to declare a first years Company profit which was considerably less than expected. This went down like a lead balloon in the City, and sent our share price tumbling.

More to the point, and the reason why I had not wanted to do it, was that we spent all that money simply to increase our overheads and give away the information we had been getting paid for on the telephone.

Today, TEAMtalk.com is a web site with lots of ads and, presumably, pays for itself, but in 1996, very few people wanted to advertise on a web site, so all we did was kill a very profitable telephone publishing product and increase our costs.

The moral of this story is that an internet site must add something positive to the business, and so the objective behind creating it must be clear.

There are now lots of web designers to choose from, and they are a lot more down to earth than the elitist few who pioneered these skills 10 or more years ago. However, finding a good one is just as difficult.

A quick way to do it is by spending a few hours on the Internet looking at sites which set out to do a similar task to that you have in mind. As long as they do not belong to a direct competitor, or have been produced in-house by the site owner, you should be able to contact the designers of any sites that impress you, and invite them in for a discussion. They often give contact details somewhere on the site.

It is also worth remembering that the image you wish to project should be reflected by the site itself. That could mean slick and professional, but not always. When I became Chairman of the Association of Second Homeowners, I decided that the last thing we wanted was a slick web site. The whole presentation had to look sincere and homely. Furthermore, it had to be very easy to read, and to navigate. The result was a site which looked somewhat amateurish, but did the job perfectly.

I have talked elsewhere about the use of copy and type faces in communication, but it is worth repeating here that the basic rules also apply to the internet. Anyone who has clicked through scores of internet sites looking for something will know how frustrating it is to navigate around a badly designed site, ploughing through unnecessary verbiage and graphics.

Keep it simple and clearly state what is on offer in readable type.

Once the site is to your liking, you must then decide how to promote it. Companies with big marketing budgets can use both traditional promotion techniques as well as search engine optimisation etc, whereas those with limited means will probably concentrate on the internet itself. However, everyone must take every opportunity to get the web address 'out there'.

Letterheads, company vehicles, promotional gifts, premises, in fact everything that can possibly carry the web address, should do so.

It is relatively easy to find out how well your site is doing in terms of hits, because the search engines now offer some sophisticated measurement tools that can not only tell you how many people are reading it, but which bits are read by what type of person.

The internet has transformed the way people shop for goods and services. Retailers have had to adapt to competitions from online traders, and the price comparison opportunities that the web provides. The clever ones use the reassurance of their name, and their distribution network to great advantage, so negating minor pricing shortfalls.

In the end, the worth of a web site can only be judged on the business it creates, so you must ensure that the products are appropriate, and the resulting business is identifiable as such.

I am not an expert on digital marketing, having had relatively little experience of it. However, it does seem to me that companies frequently put barriers in the way of potential customers by doing daft things such as making site navigation difficult, imposing cookies on web visitors, or annoying people with tediously repetitive emails.

Apply the basic rules of communication to web and email marketing, and you will give it the best possible chance of success.

# CHAPTER 12

## Public relations

"If you do appoint a PR agency, bear in mind that, unlike an ad agency, the individual you deal with on a day-to-day basis, does almost all of the work personally, and so it is important to look at what they have done in the past, rather than how successful the agency has been."

# Public Relations

Company marketing directors usually get the overall responsibility for PR, whether they want it or not. Sometimes this can involve sponsorship, which can be fun, and occasionally such things as political lobbying, which are not.

PR, like all forms of marketing, requires a clear objective if it is to be cost effective and, more importantly, accountable. At William Hill, for example, I set out to soften the perception of betting as a leisure pursuit so that we could enlarge the potential market by introducing interesting bets on sports such as golf and football. Although this inevitably also helped our competitors, it was up to us to grab the initiative, and it did mean that I could do an immediate cost/benefit analysis.

PR is often, for many Companies, just a question of getting as much free publicity as possible, so long as it is positive, and there is nothing much wrong with that as the objective.

I have on occasion decided to do it myself, rather than involve a professional PR person, for reasons outlined below. I have also had an internal PR team to draw on, and sometimes I decided the task was one for a PR Agency.

For the unwary marketer embarking on a first PR provider appointment, here's a word of caution. The Agency or Consultant you choose will undoubtedly suggest a monthly retainer. Forget it.

Agree a list of tasks, and pay per task. So if, for example, they say that, based on what they can see of your organisation, you can expect to get 6 good press stories away each year, plus 3 sponsored radio interviews, all of which will cost you £X; instead of paying that as a monthly fee, you can tell them how much they will be paid for each, as and when they are achieved.

You, of course, will need to feed the Agency with good material, and the downside of pay as you go is that you need to cultivate a nose for a story. However, if the PR people are any good, they will be around and asking questions so as to pick up anything that may make good copy.

PR, like anything else, can cause you problems, so be careful. I once employed a leading Agency to put the right spin on our massive horse racing sponsorship programme. We hired the Brewery, a conference venue in London, invited the Countries racing journalists, and one of my in house PR guys got a leading comedian to front the presentation for £2000, and a limo for the day. He turned up, pocketed the money, and asked me what I would like him to do. He's a racing man, and so already knew something about our sponsorship activities. I gave him the information that would appear on the screens, and said 'just tell a few gags around this lot'. 'Two grand doesn't get you gags!' he says. I resisted the temptation to ask him why we would want him other than to tell jokes, pulled out my cheque book, slapped it on the table and said 'your no good to me if your not going to be funny, so how much do you want?'

'Oh all right' he says 'Put it away and I'll see what I can do'.

Well, his gags had whiskers on them – he was pathetic. Fortunately, the meat of the presentation was handled by John Sanderson, at the time Clerk of York Racecourse, who was brilliant, and made our 'star' look a muppet. He, realising that he had literally been upstaged, leapt to his feet, and put on the show he should have given us in the first place.

Like every other aspect of marketing, you do need luck in PR. When I worked for a group of furniture stores with a large outlet in Manchester, the cost of advertising in the Manchester Evening News meant I had to supplement the ad expenditure with a series of PR stunts. One involved a Float in a carnival procession, which our lorry driver decided to take over the elevated Manchunian Way in order to join up with the procession – in a gale! Needless to say, half the float floated away, including the nice polystyrene pillars and the roof. I left everyone to do the best that they could with what was left, and drove back to our office in Sheffield.

Later that afternoon, our MD phoned down to say 'I see we made the front page of the Manchester Evening News, well done'. 'Look, I said, thinking he was taking the mickey, 'the idiot driving the lorry.......etc'. 'Woe', said the Boss, 'you had better come up to my office'. I walked in there to find a copy of the MEN with a photograph of our float front and centre and our name big and bold. It was an aerial shot and so if we had a roof on the float, it would never have been used.

On another occasion, when running a group of retail furnishing stores in Scotland, the outlet in Fort William was found to be riddled with dry rot. A condition of the insurance was that it be rebuilt, and so we did, and eventually I had to stage a grand reopening. Fort William today is a thriving bustling community; in 1976, it was a one horse town. However it did attract young students to work in the tourist industry, and I commandeered two very beautiful examples to act as hostesses on the opening day, dishing out champagne to the potential punters. A guy wandered in off the street and asked if he could take a photograph of the two girls. As they were bedecked in our trading name and livery, I had no objection, and the girls were only interested in getting a copy of the photograph. The following morning, a colleague produced a copy of the Daily Express, national edition, with half of the front page devoted to our two girls with our name big and bold across their chests.

I could bore you with many examples of good luck in terms of PR coverage, but it is a little like the good luck you get in business generally; the more you try, the luckier you get.

However, there are always exceptions. The Company that a colleague and I turned into a public Company had the largest automated telephone call handling system in Europe, and we decided to try for a contract to offer National Lottery entry on the phone. It had been done successfully in the USA, and we had the support of BT, who agreed to match our £50,000 bid budget, most of which would be spent on political lobbying. Obviously, age verification would be a big issue for Camelot, but my technical colleagues assured me that could be managed. Now there have been occasions when I have failed to check things out before jumping into a project, and this was one of them. After 3 months and £50,000 of PR expenditure, I was told by our people that, after all, it would not be possible to verify the age of telephone purchasers.

If you do appoint a PR agency, bear in mind that, unlike an ad agency, the person you deal with does almost all of the work personally, so it is important to look at what *they* have done in the past, rather than how successful the Agency has been. It's also worth making sure that you get along with that individual. If you don't like him or her much, they are unlikely to go down well with the people you are trying to impress.

Finally, and this applies to trade press PR activity in particular, do not be frightened to pick up the telephone and speak to the journalist who may be interested in what you have to offer. They are often as anxious to fill a page as you are to get a story away, and sometimes appreciate contact with you directly, rather than a PR person.

# CHAPTER 13

## Research

"Commissioning original qualitative research is not for the faint hearted. It can be expensive and inappropriate, though the research companies will rarely tell you that."

# Research

Research is a much maligned discipline, and rightly so.

The number of times I turn on the news to hear quotes from some research project or other, knowing full well that it is absolute rubbish put out to get free publicity for the Company or individual who published it.

A leading estate agency, for example, has in the past issued blatantly false statements about the housing market, just to attract publicity. I challenged their head of research about one such fabrication, to be told that in her opinion, Government figures, based on factual returns, were under stated, and so had been adjusted accordingly. In other words, she had made them up.

Neither should we accept everything that the government puts out, particularly if it is based on sampling. A few years ago, John Prescott's ODPM Department issued guidelines to local authorities on which they were to base an extensive and expensive piece of research. These mixed qualitative and quantitative techniques to such a degree, that the findings were useless.

Some of the data gathering methods used by the larger research Companies when analysing market trends, can also leave a lot to be desired. I was once asked for information by a Research Company looking to publish a paper on the floorcovering industry, which I could not provide, but I did give an opinion. This opinion later appeared in their Report, for which they were charging £200 per copy, as a fact, quoting 'industry sources'.

Having said all of that, some research techniques are not only worthwhile, but essential as a preface to certain major expenditures.

Well moderated group discussions can provide Companies with an invaluable insight into the mindset of potential customers, or act as a sounding board prior to embarking on a major investment programme or marketing campaign. Before commissioning designers to change a retail image, I would spend serious money on group discussions, the feedback from which was invaluable.

Desk researching existing data, including any relevant omnibus research, is an essential part of any strategic planning proposal. Even if you decide to discount the findings, it is better to state that you have done so, and give the reasons why, than to appear as if you have not considered them.

The Chartered Institute of Marketing has a decent research library, as have the British Libraries in London and Leeds.

You can use the internet to find out what has been published, and then phone around to see if anyone has a copy.

If your ad or PR agency has a research department, they may have something useful.

Commissioning original quantitative research is not for the faint hearted. It is expensive, and can be wholly inappropriate, though the research companies will rarely tell you that.

If you ever find yourself being brow beaten with quantitative sample based research findings, get hold of the research tables, and analyse them yourself. On more than one occasion, I have found on drilling down to raw data, that a 'finding' was based on such a small sample as to be meaningless. On one occasion, it was based on half a person.

I recently asked for a copy of a major piece of research carried out on behalf of a leading Regional Development Agency, which they were using to justify their existence in the face of accusations that such quangoes are a waste of public money. Sure enough, when I got past the carefully selected extracts, I found that 70% of the businesses they were supposed to be helping, did not know who they were, or what they did.

Finally, the one research technique that should be used constantly, particularly in retailing, is the 'mystery shopper'. Nothing tells you more about a business.

# CHAPTER 14

## Training

THE
ABACUS SCHOOL
FOR
CHANCELLORS

WE HAND OVER RESPONSIBILITY
FOR RUNNING THE COUNTRY'S
FINANCES TO HISTORY AND LAW GRADUATES
AND THEN WONDER WHY THEY MAKE A MESS OF IT.

"The training requirement for each member of staff should be assessed annually at appraisal time, and delivered by whatever means is nessessary."

# Training

Most large organisations have a staff training person or a training department, and they are usually responsible to the Personnel Director, who will probably be known now as the Human Resources Director. This is unfortunate, in my opinion, because one of the most important functions in any Company is staff training, and for it to be the responsibility of someone who is possibly the most unimportant member of the Board, is a shame.

How did we ever allow the wages departments to grow into Personnel, then morph into Human Resources and become the least productive and most disruptive department in any organisation, whose influence tends to be out of all proportion to any contribution, or lack of it?

I have worked with a number of personnel people who I liked immensely on a personal level, but I never found one that was worth a fraction of their cost.

I am proud to say that none of the Companies I actually ran had need of personnel people, because I made sure of it.

Training, on the other hand, is very important. The training requirement for every member of staff should be assessed each year at appraisal time, and that training delivered by whatever means is necessary.

In marketing terms, that could mean training needs in order to keep abreast of the latest developments, or to provide the addition skills needed by someone being given a different or additional responsibility.

Rarely can this training be provided in-house.

The Chartered Institute of Marketing offers a comprehensive programme of Courses as mentioned elsewhere; open to all, but at a cost.

I am constantly amazed at the lack of training provided to people taking on new roles. When my wife became a deputy head mistress,

I asked her what training had been arranged for her, The answer was nothing. She was expected to take on a management role without any preparation whatsoever, just because she had proved herself to be a good infant teacher.

The same thing happens in Boardrooms throughout the land, and as for Government! We hand over responsibility for running the Countries finances to history and law graduates, without any formal financial or management training or experience, and then we wonder why they make a mess of it.

# CHAPTER 15

## Customer relationship management

"Do not confuse the provision of customer information with harassment."

# Customer Relationship Management

This used to be known as customer service, but so many factors have entered the equation, it really does deserve its beefed up title.

Getting customer relationships right will earn you very few accolades from those who benefit most, but get it wrong and you can literally ruin your Company, making all your efforts in other directions superfluous.

I do not intend to repeat all the good stuff available elsewhere on how to organise call centres, train sales staff etc, but will concentrate on the marketing decisions made for other, and often valid, reasons of profitability, that can have a severe and detrimental effect on the way that customers perceive a Company.

A most important thing, in my view, is not to confuse the provision of customer information with harassment. It was bad enough in the days when buying from certain companies triggered a deluge of postal mail, but now that we have the internet, that can become a time consuming flood of offers which actually create a powerful dislike of the company responsible, in the minds of the potential customers. So, the requirement is to keep contact down to meaningful messages, preferably targeted towards known preferences, and not to be tempted into duplicating the messages 'just in case'.

Another aspect of relationship management that customers dislike is the obvious rip-off, and care should be taken when looking for ways to increase profit margins, that customers will see as just that.

The car industries are the worst offenders in this. In fact, the last thing some of them have is 'respect' for their customers. How do they expect people to react when they see a 500% mark up on the cost of oil used in a service, for example? It is not as if it is hard to compare the price of a litre of oil, so everyone can see what they are up to.

And, while on the subject of cars, how do these manufacturers justify the fact that customers in other Countries can purchase an identical car at considerably less than the UK price? A Supercharged Range Rover is built in Solihull, and exported to the US to sell for $94000. The same car, bought at a local dealer a few miles from the factory, will cost £80,000, equivalent to $130,000 at the time of writing with the exchange rate at $1.63. Even allowing for our higher taxation, that could be seen as a rip off.

Not that Land Rover are the worst offenders. I have used them as an example only because their cars are built here, and so they have none of the usual excuses such as shipping, or the cost of producing right hand drive vehicles. It's no secret that the UK is known in the motor trade as 'treasure island'.

I believe that the car companies get away with this because the motor trade is the only retail industry dominated by manufacturers, rather than retailers.

We all know that retail competition keeps prices down, although fine margins tend to mean bargain prices but little in the way of customer service. However, in some cases – technology products, brown, and white goods, for example – this has re-created a market for the specialist retailer. Some people will pay a specialist local outfit considerably more than a high street multiple for the same item, in exchange for some old fashioned service.

Telephony providers have given less and less service as their margins were squeezed, and taken advantage of their customers in the process, so they are now seen as a commodity by many people. Were it not for the in-built hassle involved in switching from one supplier to another, the telecommunications churn rate would be even greater than it is.

Banks have gone much the same way, and now that everyone knows what a bunch of overpaid chancers they are, any notions of customer loyalty are a thing of the past.

To sum up, many an opportunity to create a bond with customers has been squandered by organisations who should have known better, and, in my opinion, it will come around and bite them in the bum.

Loyalty schemes, such as cards, can create a very mercenary brand of loyalty, but at least they are targeted at existing customers.

Let's face it, when times are tough, companies do have to 'buy business'.

Restricting attractive promotions to new customers, thereby running the risk of antagonising the people who are currently paying the wages, will almost always prove to be counter productive. If it is a product aimed at a totally new type of customer, and offering something completely new, there is no need to restrict it anyway. Offering something that would benefit existing customers, but only to new customers, is asking to be seen as a Company that does not value its business. The best way to create loyalty is to use add-on marketing techniques to get more out of your existing customer base, and do it in such a way that it also creates good will. Done well, a loyalty scheme need not be promoted beyond existing customers, because the word will get around. Never underestimate the ability of your customers to create more customers simply by what is said in day to day conversation. This does not even require a 'recommend a friend' offer. Having said that, for some reason 'recommend a friend' often works in product areas which are male dominated. Men must be more mercenary than women.

Sometimes simply making customers feel welcome is enough.

There's a hand written sign outside a wonderful country Coop shop in the Langdale Valley, where every other house is a holiday let, which says 'Customers wanted. Apply within. Training given. Must have own money'.

I watch people smile, and then go in to see what it has to offer.

# ........AND A FEW OTHER THINGS

A.   Joining the Board

B.   Office politics and relationships

C.   MBI's, MBO's, and BIMBO's

D.   Advertising Headlines by Claude
    Hopkins – extracted from his book
    *Scientific Advertising.*

CHAIRMAN   CHIEF EXECUTIVE   H.R. DIRECTOR   I.T. DIRECTOR   FINANCE DIRECTOR   MARKETING DIRECTOR

# A. Joining the Board

In the 70's, a hot topic in the marketing magazines was the lack of marketing people at Board level. These days, a hot topic in the marketing magazines is the lack of marketing people at Board level.

In my opinion, the reason for the lack of marketing people at Board level, is the same now as it was then – most marketing people do not understand finance, and would patently struggle to make a contribution at Board Meetings. I believe most of them desire a directorship for its status, rather than the added responsibility, and it shows.

Until such time as these marketers wake up to what is required from a Company Director, and identify the contribution they need to make, no Board will see any reason to appoint them.

Marketing people tend to be creative rather than numerate. That is fine up until the time when the marketer wants to become a Board Member. He must then acquire a basic fundamental knowledge of how to 'read' a set of accounts. That does not mean buying a book which explains balance sheets and statutory accounts, useful as that can be. The most important statistics at any Board Meeting are the Management Accounts. They should show what is really going on in the business and, if they are well structured, what needs attention. If they do not do that, someone needs to have a conversation with the Financial Director.

Director or not, the person responsible for the marketing function, ideally needs to see the monthly figures in order to do the job. Some Companies are loathe to issue such confidential information outside of Board Members, which may provide the best reason for a marketer to become a Director.

Once appointed, the Marketing Director, like all executive Board Members, will usually be expected to produce a Board Report seven days ahead of Meetings. This is then included in the Board Papers issued to all Directors prior to each Meeting, so that views can be formulated and questions prepared. The danger is self evident. It is simply not acceptable to float an ill thought through idea at a Board Meeting, so any new proposal must be well researched and presented, and, most importantly, has to fit into the existing financial projections, or clearly show why and how they must change. Any proposal for additional marketing expenditure, for example, should quantify the financial benefit that will accrue from it. Then expect that both expenditure and benefit will be incorporated into the budgets.

Whatever a marketer may think about accountants, he or she must make every effort to cultivate the Financial Director as an ally. The FD can help a non-financial person to understand the Accounts, particularly if it is obvious that person is trying to help themselves. Any proposals can be discussed informally, and most FD's of my acquaintance were flattered to be included in that thinking process.

When looking for advancement, marketing people should sell themselves like they sell products and services - features and benefits. Just make sure that those include knowing how to add up!

## B. Office Politics and Relationships

I'm pleased to say that almost every political 'animal' I have had the misfortune to come up against in business, eventually got their comeuppance. These people are the scourge of business life.

I blame ego driven CEO's who enjoy the flattery and ignore the harm these insecure people can do. I have seen one Public Company ruined by politics and over the years, I have known scores of talented people who changed employer in order to get away from the pressures such activity creates. I hate health-and-safety-at-work idiots who go on about 'bullying' in the workplace, but that's what office politics are – an insidious form of bullying.

I confess that I have never found an answer to it, and can only rejoice in that I no longer have to put up with it. I usually tried to ignore attacks, hoping that my 'boss' at the time would see through it, but that rarely works because the 'boss' is either too busy, or is daft enough to fall for having his ego stroked, usually the latter. In my first 'big' job I had a Chairman who was so confident of his position and his abilities that, after he promoted me above a whole lot of people who he knew would instantly hate my guts, put aside the hate mail addressed to him about me, and brought it into my office once a week to discuss. It should have taught me how to avoid antagonising people, but all it did was give me a false sense of security, because I thought every big boss would be as sensible.

There have been times when things have gotten so bad, I almost decided to join in, but I always concluded that being able to look at myself in the mirror each morning had more going for it than the satisfaction of shafting someone who deserved it.

We can, of course, find ourselves sucked into a political situation without knowing it, and that's happened to me on more than one occasion. All you can do is be true to yourself and, again, hope that other people realise what's going on.

The worse thing you can do is constantly look over your shoulder, because that's when you either get decisions wrong, or stop making them.

The 'political' story that often comes to mind also sparked my distrust of non-executive directors generally, and non-executive chairmen in particular – but more of that elsewhere.

I was managing director of an advertising agency in 1988, which I had rescued from near insolvency after first receiving approval to my plans from an insolvency practitioner (this, in case you ever need to know, is the way a difficult turnaround should be approached – get permission to trade from an insolvency practitioner, then a good financial director alongside you and, most important, make sure the director's indemnity insurance is up to date). A chap I knew in a major venture capital Company had noted my efforts, and thought I could do us both a favour by taking over a poorly performing ad agency investment of his, and merging it with the Company I was running. I would restructure the combined entity to increase efficiency, reduce overheads, and we should then be in profit.

Obviously, I pointed out, there would be people I did not need, and top of that list was the expensive non-executive chairman of his investment, who had put money into it, but had also presided over the mess I needed to sort out. However, I did reluctantly agree that this individual could continue as a non-executive director in the new set up, albeit on a vastly reduced salary.

We arranged a meeting of the two Boards at a neutral venue. My venture capital friend thought it would be a good idea if he stayed out of the way for this initial get together, assuring me that everyone knew and agreed the changes I wished to make.

Five minutes into the meeting, after I had announced the new Board structure, I realised that our venture capitalist had sold me short. The first that their existing chairman knew of his demotion was when I told him about it, and he was not pleased. In fact, he made it clear that he had no intention of stepping down. As that was a deal breaker, as far as I was concerned, the meeting broke up in stony silence.

That man declared war on me, and over the ensuing months made a real nuisance of himself, with our clients, our suppliers, and my colleagues. The venture capitalist ran scared and simply let his investment disappear into insolvency. He never did own up to our agreement.

I made an enemy I did not want, through no fault of mine, simply because I trusted someone to do the right thing – a lesson you should note, dear reader.

That weak kneed investor, incidentally, went on to become a senior director in one of the largest venture capitalist organisations in the World, which says all you need to know about venture capitalists.

Office relationships are always interesting. The kind that can get people into trouble were summed up to me by one Chairman who, faced with sorting out a situation where a married male manager and a married female manager had begun a relationship that would inevitably end with one of them deciding to leave, said "why do they have to take seriously what they should be poking in fun?".

Business friendships rarely develop into more lasting relationships, but are no less enjoyable or fruitful for that. However, I am still friends with, and see regularly, people who I worked for, and some who worked for me. It's nothing to be ashamed of, after all, you often spend more time with your colleagues than you do with your family.

Some people let you down, but it's better to remain optimistic about office relationships than to view everyone with suspicion. Relationships with suppliers and clients are something else again but can also be enjoyable, provided no one tries to take advantage.

The current weapon of choice for the office politician is the Email. I was lucky enough to spend most of my working life in an Email free environment. Before the email, it was the internal memo, but that was never as potent as the ability to invade someone's inbox with enough documents to waste half of their day. Every CEO should make it clear to the staff that sending a copy of everything to everybody in the organisation as an arse covering exercise, will be viewed as time wasting, and merit a written warning.

## MBI's MBO's & BIMBO's.

A marketing person should always be on the lookout for the big opportunity, the chance to make what is known as 'f\*\*ck you' money. This usually involves acquiring ownership of, or a shareholding in, a business of a reasonable size, which has the potential for value to be added, and with a view to an eventual trade sale or floatation. For many people that means buying the Company they work for. However, it is worth saying at the outset that any business with an initial turnover of less than £20million is unlikely to offer sufficient potential for the deal to attract venture capital, and this is the usual method of funding.

Buying the Company you work for is a management buy out (MBO). Buying one that you do not work for is a management buy in (MBI).

A combination of the two is known as a buy in/ management buy out (BIMBO).

As few of us have the spare cash to buy a Company of any size, the deals are usually financed by venture capital. However, the starting point for any would be entrepreneur is almost always either a firm of corporate lawyers or, more often, an accountancy practice with a corporate finance department. Whichever you choose to approach must have relevant experience, a track record of successfully completing deals, and you should only talk to a senior partner in the first instance, for obvious reasons of confidentiality. They may tell you that your project is a non-runner, and if it's an MBO you are considering, you cannot then be sure it is safe to broach the subject with your employer. However, don't give up after only one negative opinion, because other advisors may have a different view.

It is always a good idea to bounce the project off of a few advisors before deciding which of them you would like to work with, bearing in mind that doing a deal will involve spending many hours with them and things can get very stressful. However, do bear in mind that these people talk to each other, and if you speak to too many of them, you will quickly be seen to be 'hawking it around'.

You should initially expect all of the people you approach to test the viability of the project, because, if they are prepared to take it on, it will likely be on a 'double or nothing' basis- either the deal goes ahead and they are paid double their normal fee, or it doesn't, and they get nothing.

A common sticking point is that they like the deal, but insist that the management team is strengthened, perhaps in terms of financial expertise, for example. You must then find the additional personnel, or go elsewhere in the hope that other people will not insist upon the same. If this problem arises, don't let anyone force someone of their choice on to you. They all have a database of would be buy in candidates, but doing an MBI or BIMBO with someone you do not know would be like marrying a stranger.

In fact, without getting up anyone's nose, you must make sure that you stay in control of everything that goes on, right from the start, which is what I will try to help you do in writing this.

Once you have a lawyer and accountant on board, a detailed business plan must be produced, usually by the accountants. Preparing this will take up a good deal of your time, but is worth agonising over because any deal will be based on it, and you will be expected to achieve the projected figures shown in it.

Then it's time to look for financial backing. Your advisors will know all of the potential investors, and will usually set up a 'beauty parade'. This involves meeting with a number of venture capitalist organisations, who will tell you all about themselves, and to whom you will be expected to present your business plan. At this stage you are in the driving seat, but only if you and your proposition impresses the VC's. Their offers may vary, and it is up to you which one, or ones, to choose. Some may be for a set term, for example, so forcing an exit date on you, whereas some will be open ended.

Rarely will one VC pick up the whole investment. You may have a lead investor, with two or three others taking smaller stakes.

There could be a requirement for mezzanine finance, and you will definitely need 'banking'. This brings traditional bankers into the mix, who may look for 'kickers', or small equity stakes, realised on exit.

Without going into too much detail, I am trying to give you some idea of what the process involves, and how much time you will need to devote to it, bearing in mind that you will also have a 'day job'.

By now you should have an idea of how much you can afford to pay, and it is time to approach the Company you wish to buy with an indicative offer. Anything can then happen, and often does. In our case a competing offer from a Public Company had to be fended off under Stock Exchange Rules.

It can easily take six months to do a deal, during which time you may be running the Company which you hope to buy. The dangers are obvious.

In return for investing in you, VC Companies want to make a big return, known as the Internal Rate of Return, or IRR. They will look for regular interest payments, annual dividends, and capital appreciation, which could also involve regularly stripping the Company of any 'surplus funds' generated, which they consider to be spare cash. Don't let them screw this down too tightly, or you could end up borrowing additional funds to buy something that should be purchased out of cash flow.

All of this you will need to consider as you go through the process, but do take note of the contracted repayments involved and be confident that you can make them. Miss one, and you could find your shareholding diluted.

The VC's will also require a commitment from you, which could mean money up front in return for shares, and a charge against your assets, which usually means your house. Just remember that these things are negotiable. You will not get away without any commitment, as the investors will want to make sure that you have a big incentive to make it work, but you can stop them from going overboard. When we did our buyout, I told the lead investor that I was only prepared to put up half of what they wanted me to pay for my shares, which they eventually agreed to, and which avoided

my needing a loan. You can expect to receive shares worth vastly more than the money you put up, it is known as a leveraged buy out. However, the institutions will also receive preference shares, making your shareholding worth little until you have found a way for them to redeem their 'prefs'.

Get your accountants to break down all of the deal offers so that you can understand what each expects you to do in order to get you to your eventual pay day. You need to be confident that you can achieve the requirements, or you could loose everything. Our lead investor sent us off to visit a Company that they were already invested in, on the pretext that we could perhaps do business with them in the future. It quickly became apparent that we were really there to see what happened to management teams that fail to fulfil their obligations, as the Company had recently installed a new Chairman and CEO, the previous incumbents having been demoted after failing to achieve target, and had their shareholdings severely diluted.

The thing you must remember throughout the deal process is that all the people involved probably went through the same things with another investment last week, or the week before, not that you would ever guess by the way everything is debated and argued over, sometimes late into the night. At 2 am one morning we were sat in a meeting room listening to two lawyers argue the toss, when one turned to my colleague and said "Don't worry, this is just legal masturbation", to which my colleague replied "Yes, I was beginning to realise you were a bunch of wankers!" Fortunately, they took it in good part, unlike the lady lawyer representing the potential Bankers, who decided at midnight during one boisterous meeting that she'd had enough, and called a cab to take her home – from Leeds to Edinburgh!

Now for the most important thing I have to say about the whole process.

Bearing in mind that the 'professionals' will only get paid if the deal is done, don't worry too much about the seemingly endless meetings. When their fee meters have clocked up a serious amount of money, the pressure is on *them* to do the deal. At that stage, you are in a strong position to resist calls for you to accept less. As the finer points of the deal are put in place, you may be asked, for example, to take less salary, waive your right to dividends etc in order to 'expedite the deal'. If the cumulated fees are high enough, you just say no, and there is little they can do about it. I would like to say that we knew enough to stand our ground, but at that time, we didn't, and it cost us our dividend entitlement for 5 years.

However, we did benefit from having a lawyer who looked after our interests when it came to thrashing out the small print. For example, a section of the investment agreement that should have said we were entitled to cars 'up to the value of' actually said 'at least to the value of', which cheered me up no end.

One issue that must be faced is that of non-executive directors on your Board.

The institutions will want one or two non-execs looking after their interest, and they will submit people to you for consideration. You must agree to this, so just make sure that you can work with the people you choose, and that they can potentially bring something to the party, other than simply acting as a watchdog for the investors.

Non-execs can be very useful. The good ones have a lot of experience, and they are well connected. However, you may be pressured to accept one as a non-executive Chairman. DON'T! If you do, the first time your new Chairman takes his seat at the top of your boardroom table and calls the meeting to order, you realise that you have a tiger by the tail.

The easy way to avoid this is to carve up the key positions amongst your management team, so that imposing a Chairman on you would cause an obvious problem.

You may find this strange, coming from someone who has held a number of Chairmanships on a non-executive basis, but you will find my reasons elsewhere.

Once the deal is done, and you have signed the documents, things get back to normal. Apart from a monthly Board Meeting attended by the non-execs, for which you ensure that everything is on budget, you will be left to get on with it.

Hopefully, despite making sure that you didn't get stitched up, you will have made a good impression on everyone concerned, because you never know what may happen down the line, and you may need their goodwill.

Eventually, you should get to a point in the development of your business when you can look for a way to engineer an exit for your investors. It could be a trade sale, or floatation. Look carefully at the options because some may benefit the institutions far more than you.

Doing a buy out or buy in deal is a big hassle, and some people can't take it. However, for those who pull it off, it frequently leads to serious wealth and financial security.

## D.  Advertising Headlines by Claude Hopkins

– an extract from his book *Scientific Advertising*.

# Chapter 5

# Headlines

The difference between advertising and personal salesmanship lies largely in personal contact. The salesman is there to avoid personal attention. He cannot be ignored. The advertisement can be ignored. But the salesman wastes much of his time on prospects whom he can never hope to interest. He cannot pick them out. The advertisement is read only by interested people who, by their very own volition, study what we have to say. The purpose of a headline is to pick out people you can interest. You wish to talk to someone in a crowd. So the first thing you say is, "hey there, Bill Jones" to get the right persons attention. So it is with an advertisement. What you have will interest certain people only, and for certain reasons. You care only for those people. Then create a headline which will hail those people only.

Perhaps a blind headline or some clever conceit will attract many times as many. But they may consist of mostly impossible subjects for what you have to offer. And the people you are after may never realize that the ad refers to something they may want.

Headlines on ads are like headlines on news items. Nobody reads a whole newspaper. One is interested in financial news, one in political, one in society, one in cookery, one in sports, etc. There are whole pages in any newspaper which we may never scan at all. Yet other people might turn directly to those pages. We pick out what we wish to read by headlines, and we don't want those headlines misleading. The writing of headlines is one of the greatest journalistic arts. They either conceal or reveal an interest.

Suppose a newspaper article stated that a certain woman was the most beautiful in the city. That article would be of intense interest to that woman and her friends. But neither she nor her friends would ever read it if the headline was "Egyptian Psychology". So in advertising. It is commonly said that people do not read advertisements. That is silly, of course. We who spend millions in advertising and watch the returns marvel at the readers we get. Again and again we see 20 percent of all the readers of a newspaper cut out a certain coupon. But people do not read ads for amusement. They don't read ads which, at a glance, seem to offer nothing interesting. A double-page ad on women's dresses will not gain a glance from a man. Nor will a shaving cream ad from a woman.

Always bear these facts in mind. People are hurried. The average person worth cultivating has too much to read. They skip three-fourths of the reading matter which they pay to get. They are not going to read your business talk unless you make it worth their while and let the headline show it.

People will not be bored in print. They may listen politely at a dinner table to boasts and personalities, life history etc. But in print they choose their own companions, their own subjects. They want to be amused or benefited. They want economy, beauty, labor savings, good things to eat and wear. There may be products which interest them more than anything else in the magazine. But they will never know it unless the headline or picture tells them.

## Scientific Advertising

The writer of this chapter spends far more time on headlines than on writing. He often spends hours on a single headline. Often scores of headlines are discarded before the right one is selected. For the entire return from an ad depends on attracting the right sort of readers. The best of salesmanship has no chance whatever unless we get a hearing. The vast difference in headlines is shown by keyed returns which this book advocates. The identical ad run with various headlines differs tremendously in its returns. It is not uncommon for a change in headlines to multiply returns from five or ten times over.

So we compare headlines until we know what sort of appeal pays best. That differs in every line, of course. The writer has before him keyed returns on nearly two thousand headlines used on a single product. The story in these ads are nearly identical. But the returns vary enormously, due to the headlines. So with every keyed return in our record appears the headlines that we used. Thus we learn what type of headline has the most widespread appeal. The product has many uses. It fosters beauty. It prevents disease. It aids daintiness and cleanliness. We learn to exactness which quality most of our readers seek. This does not mean we neglect the others. One sort of appeal may bring half the returns of another, yet be important enough to be profitable. We overlook no field that pays. But we know what proportion of our ads should, in the headline, attract any certain class.

For this same reason we employ a vast variety of ads. If we are using twenty magazines we may use twenty separate ads. This because circulation's overlap, and because a considerable percentage of people are attracted by each of several forms of approach. We wish to reach them all.

## Claude C. Hopkins

On a soap, for instance, the headline "Keep Clean" might attract a very small percentage. It is too commonplace. So might the headline, "No Animal Fat". People may not care much about that. The headline, "it Floats" might prove interesting. But a headline referring to beauty or complexion might attract many times as many. An automobile ad might refer in the headline to a good universal joint. It might fall flat, because so few buyers think of universal joints. The same ad with a headline, "The Sportiest of Sport Bodies", might out pull the other fifty to one.

This is enough to suggest the importance of headlines. Anyone who keys ads will be amazed at the difference. The appeals we like best will rarely prove best, because we do not know enough people to average up their desires. So we learn on each line by experiment.

But back of all lie fixed principles. You are presenting an ad to millions. Among them is a percentage, small or large, whom you hope to interest. Go after that percentage and try to strike the chord that responds. If you are advertising corsets, men and children don't interest you. If you are advertising cigars, you have no use for non-smokers. Razors won't attract women, rouge will not interest men.

Don't think that those millions will read your ads to find out if your product interests. They will decide at a glance – by your headline or your pictures. Address the people you seek, and them only.